Contents

KU-446-347

Introduction

Traditional methods of teaching science and many people's secondary school experience can lead to early science experiences becoming formal, restrictive and uninspiring. Science is not about lab coats, Bunsen burners or formal 'experiments' especially in early years. It is about young children making sense of the world around them using all of their five senses.

Early science should inspire children to explore, investigate and ask questions of their world. It should encourage curiosity and problem solving. With this in mind, science probably more than many other areas of learning, is dependent upon the quality of the learning environment provided. Resources and play experiences need to invite children to interact with them and be open enough for children to guide their own learning journeys.

The activities in this book are not, therefore a list of 'experiments' to be completed and ticked off. They are suggestions for play experiences which can, with a little planning, be provided to excite and inspire children and which happen to offer the chance to explore and build on early science understanding. Children learn much more about floating and sinking if they are having a go at trying to sink a raft with pebbles or playing with ice boats than they ever would ploughing through a pile of objects to identify which ones float and which sink. I have also included a few 'Wow!' activities designed to get children talking and asking questions and to show that science is far from boring.

The important thing to remember when providing science exploration both indoors and outdoors is that the children are making sense of their own world (not yours)! They need to try things themselves, explore their own questions and try things out without adults interfering to give a textbook view of what's right or wrong.

The outdoor environment offers children a unique chance to engage with nature and the elements and to explore activities which would not make sense transposed indoors. It is important that practitioners embrace these opportunities and make sure that children are able to explore and investigate outdoors in all weathers. The book offers ideas for outdoor learning come rain, shine or snow, I really hope you enjoy exploring them alongside the children. And remember: 'The best kept classroom and the richest cupboard are roofed only by the sky.' (Margaret McMillan)

Skin allergy alert

Some detergents and soaps can cause skin reactions.

Always be mindful of potential skin allergies when letting children mix anything with their hands and always provide lots of facilities to wash materials off after they have been in contact with the skin. Watch out for this symbol on the relevant pages!

Food allergy alert

FOOD allergy !

When using food stuffs to enhance your outdoor play opportunties always be mindful of potential food allergies. We have used this symbol on the relevant pages.

Raft sinkers

What you need:

- Pipe cleaners
- A wide selection of sticks
- Outdoor water tray
- A selection of small toys
- Pebbles

What to do:

1. Set up the water tray outdoors.
2. Show the children how to weave pipe cleaners in and out of the sticks to create wooden rafts.
3. Let the children explore floating their wooden rafts in the water tray.
4. Ask: Can you float one of your toys on the raft?
5. Using the toys and or the pebbles can you see if you can sink the raft?

Taking it forward

- Try making bigger or smaller rafts using different sized sticks. Does a heavier raft sink?
- Have a competition to see who can get the most pebbles on their raft before it tips or sinks.

What's in it for the children?

This is a really fun way for children to explore floating as part of their ongoing play and investigation rather than a boring 'will this float/ will this sink?' type activity which is uninspiring for both children and adults alike!

 Health & Safety
Always supervise children around water.

Floating building platforms

What you need:

- Old swimming pool floats
- Wooden building blocks
- Outdoor water tray

What to do:

1. Set up the water tray outdoors.
2. Position the swimming float in the water tray to provide a floating platform.
3. Encourage the children to try building towers with the wooden blocks on top of their floating platforms.
4. Ask: How high can you build your tower?
5. What happens to the blocks when they fall in the water?

Taking it forward

- Cut some old pool float 'noodles' into sections and build with floating building blocks.
- Try making patterns on floating platforms.

What's in it for the children?

Science is about children making sense of their world as they play. This activity helps children to explore floating and sinking as part of construction play in a fun and exciting new way. It takes a typical indoor activity and gives it a great outdoor twist.

 Health & Safety
Always supervise children around water.

Paddling pool bubble magic

What you need:

- A small inflatable paddling pool
- A selection of hula hoops of different sizes
- Lots of bubble solution

What to do:

1. Fill your paddling pool with a good amount of bubble mixture.
2. Show the children how to dip the hoopla hoops into the mixture, then carefully lift them out and move them around like giant bubble wands to make enormous bubbles.
3. How long can you make your big bubbles?
4. Allow the children time to explore the bubble mixture with their hoops.

Taking it forward

- Make shaped big bubble wands from old wire coat hangers and try to make different-shaped bubbles.
- Let the children stand in the paddling pool and make a big bubble come up around them. (Be careful to put a non slip surface in the middle of the pool so they don't fall over — an old floor carpet tile is ideal.)

What's in it for the children?

Children learn best about the ways materials behave by playing with them. Exploring with big bubbles helps to encourage talk about bubbles, colour, air and the wind at the same time as having lots of fun. The scale of this activity makes it unique to the outdoor environment and excellent for building on children's mathematical vocabulary about size.

 **Health & Safety**
Always supervise children around water.

Ice gloves

What you need:

- Some rubber or latex gloves
- Pegs
- A washing line
- Water
- Access to a freezer or ideally outdoors over night

What to do:

1. Fill the gloves with water and either tie off at the wrists and pop in the freezer or peg them to a washing line and leave outdoors to freeze overnight if cold enough. The outdoors method gives you a flat surface when finished as opposed to the rounded freezer version.

2. Use coloured water in some gloves for added interest.

3. When frozen, carefully remove the glove to reveal the ice hands (if you can get the fingers to bend a bit in the freezer you will have great looking ice sculptures).

4. Place the ice hands in the sand tray, on the grass or in the water tray to see what happens as the ice melts.

Taking it forward

- Freeze sequins, glitter and beads in the water to add extra sensory interest.

- Try leaving gloves made of other materials out overnight to freeze. How have they changed? Try wool, leather etc.

- Hang woollen socks of different shapes and sizes out on a washing line over night. What happens to them?

What's in it for the children?

Children need lots of opportunity to explore materials with their senses. This is a lovely and unusual tactile experience where children can explore freezing and melting.

Top tip ⭐

Try soaking objects in water before hanging them out overnight. Providing there is a frost, they will be a lot stiffer in the morning.

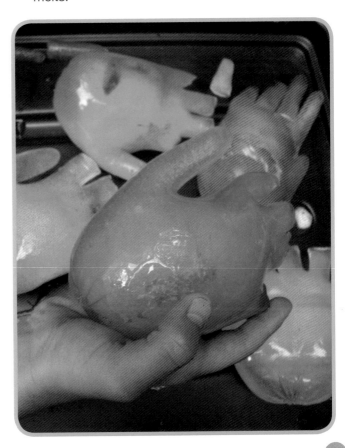

Spider web frame

What you need:

- Some small sticks
- One longer more robust stick
- Some string or wire

What to do:

1. Tie or wire four of the shorter sticks together to form a diamond or square shape, then tie or wire this to the top of the longer stick.

2. Place the long stick in the ground somewhere near to plants, flowers or bushes and wait. Eventually spiders should begin to use it at a frame for making their webs.

3. This is great for observing at any time of year but specially on cold frosty mornings or when they are covered in dew first thing on a summer's morning.

4. Encourage children to look closely without touching the web. Can they spy any other webs around the setting?

5. Encourage lots of discussion and exploration of fact books to find out about spiders.

Taking it forward

- Search for other insects or build a big insect habitat (old sand or water tray filled with soil and leaf mould) and add worms etc.

- Make up spotter bags (children's gardening tool bags filled with pencils, pens, spotter books and magnifying glasses).

- Sprinkle talc on spider webs (make sure there are no spiders in them) and touch them onto a piece of black sugar paper to give a web print.

- Why not try building an insect hotel (see *The Little Book of Minibeast Hotels* by Ann Roberts (Featherstone) to encourage even more small visitors to your outdoor area?

What's in it for the children?

Children need to be encouraged to explore their natural surrounding and to develop a respect and understanding for the creatures they share it with. Children are able to observe nature first hand in its own environment. This also provides an opportunity to encourage children to explore non-fiction books to find even more information to enhance their observations.

Ice mountain

What you need:

- **Access to a freezer** (or a bag of supermarket ice cubes)
- **Ice cube trays**
- **A water tray**
- **Salt**
- **Water**
- **Food colouring**
- **Jugs and small cups**

What to do:

1. Make lots of ice cubes (or alternatively buy a bag of ice cubes from the supermarket).

2. Pile them into a huge mountain shape in the tray.

3. Sprinkle a little bit of salt over the pile (the ice will melt a little and then refreeze together to form a big lump of ice cubes). You can add more ice cubes and repeat the process to make your ice mountain even bigger.

4. Mix some water with different food colourings. Add salt to some of the water and use both cold and warm (not hot) water.

5. Encourage children to drizzle the coloured water mixes over the ice mountain from the top. Watch as the colour drizzles down through the ice. What happens when you pour on salty or warm water?

6. Encourage children to explore the ice and see if they can find ways to melt it, colour it and so on.

Taking it forward

- Try building an ice mountain with small objects frozen into some of the cubes. Can the children work out how to get them out?

- Build a big ice tower by freezing ice in the bottom of milk cartons or margarine tubs to make big ice bricks.

What's in it for the children?

This is a great way of encouraging children to explore with their senses while investigating mixing materials together in an unusual way.

Top tip ⭐

Sprinkle the salt evenly and sparingly to get the best refreeze.

What you need:

- A metal or plastic container
- A wide selection of natural materials including leaves, flowers, petals, grasses, ferns etc.
- Water
- String
- Access to a freezer or outdoors overnight to freeze

What to do:

1. Lay your selection of leaves, flowers, etc in the bottom of your container.

2. Top the container up with water. Lay a loop of string over the edge of the container so one end is in the water and the other is outside.

3. Put the container in the freezer or leave it out overnight if there is likely to be a frost.

4. Once frozen, the ice can be removed from the container and hung up by the string loop.

5. As the light catches the ice it will shine through and show up the colours of the objects inside.

6. Hang from a tree or fence so you can observe what happens over time (be careful not to hang where children pass underneath as the sculpture will drop off its string eventually when it melts).

Top tip ⭐

If you let your string loop run to the centre of your tray it will stay on your ice hanging for longer.

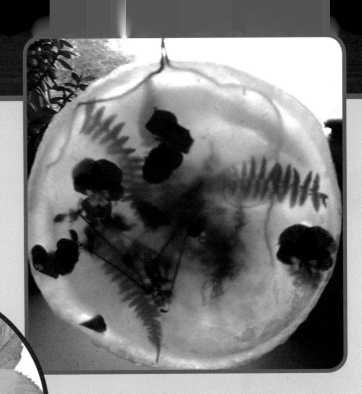

Taking it forward

- Work together to make a big ice sculpture using a large dustbin lid or round washing-up bowl and leaving it out overnight to freeze, then turn out onto the ground in the morning.

What's in it for the children?

This is an interesting way for children to blend creativity as well as exploring freezing and melting. As part of their investigations they are able to explore lots of natural materials as well as observing first hand how the ice behaves.

Super shiny water play

What you need:

- **A water play tray**
- **Tin foil**
- **A selection of coloured glass beads** (available from craft shops or online)
- **Coloured Cellophane** (from craft shops) **or recycle sweet wrappers**
- **Coloured Perspex** (scrap stores often have this type of material) **or cut up plastic drinks bottles into shapes**

What to do:

1. This is an activity which is most effective on a sunny day.

2. Cover the bottom of the tray with tin foil and fill with water.

3. Encourage the children to explore placing the coloured objects into the water. Some will float and some will sink. As the floating shapes filter the light, colours will be reflected in the bottom of the tray. The glass beads will reflect the light as will the foil. Encourage lots of talk about light, colours, reflections and patterns.

Taking it forward

- Try adding blank CDs to the water. What do they do to the sunlight? Stick coloured shapes of Cellophane to windows or a clear Perspex easel and watch what happens as the light passes through.

What's in it for the children?

This is a lovely way of combining water play with early exploration of light, colour and reflection. It is great for exploring early shape and colour language too.

frosty day box

What you need:

- A suitable container
- Paintbrushes
- Food colouring
- Spray bottles
- Salt (coloured if possible)
- Mirrors

What to do:

1. On a really frosty day make all of the above equipment available and encourage children to explore their surroundings.

2. Demonstrate how to paint on frost with warm water.

3. Spray coloured water onto frosty surfaces to make frosty rainbows.

4. Sprinkle salt on frost and watch what happens (be careful on re-frozen ground as it can be really slippery). Sprinkle coloured salt in patterns on the frost.

5. Explore breathing on mirrors, watching as warm breath mists the mirror. Try mark making on the mirrors.

Taking it forward

- Try making weather boxes for all types of weather – windy, sunny, foggy, rainy, snowy etc.

What's in it for the children?

It is really important that children make sense of their surroundings and the seasonal changes which affect them. Having ready-made weather boxes means you can react instantly to whatever the weather may bring.

Top tip ⭐

Put coloured salt into dispensers to be able to trickle in patterns on the ground or frosty surfaces.

Foggy day box

What you need:

- A suitable container
- **Fluorescent safety bands and lights** (available in pound shops)
- **Flashing bicycle lights** (red and white)
- Glow sticks
- Torches
- Mirrors
- **Glow objects and toys** (similar to those you would have in a dark den box)
- Binoculars

What to do:

1. On really foggy days explore what you can see and how far you can see.
2. Foggy weather offers a great natural opportunity to explore lights and reflection outdoors.
3. Can the children see the torches or the flashing lights? Which ones show up best?
4. Try different coloured glow sticks. Which colour shows up best?

Taking it forward

- Try exploring using high visibility safety jackets. Can the children see their friends better when they are wearing them? Get lots of mini glow sticks and make bracelets, necklaces and crowns and enjoy playing in the fog.
- Carefully cut open a glow stick (adult only) and pour the contents into a jar. Put the lid firmly onto the jar and shake. Try hanging your glow jars from a tree.

What's in it for the children?

Often the only chance young children get to explore light and reflection is in a dark den situation. This activity gives children a fun way of exploring light in the outdoor environment without the need for dark den making.

Gloves in water

What you need:

- A wide selection of gloves made from lots of different materials. Include rubber, latex (be aware of latex allergies), wool, leather, fabric (gardening gloves), coated DIY gloves, ski gloves etc
- A full water tray

What to do:

1. Encourage children to explore the water tray while wearing the gloves. Which are the best gloves for playing in the water and why?

2. Encourage lots of descriptive words such as wet, soggy, cold, dry etc.

Top tip ⭐

Try using warm water so children can really feel it as it comes through the gloves.

Taking it forward

- Offer a science challenge to the children to help encourage exploration. A letter from Santa asking which gloves will keep his hands dry in the snow is always popular.

- Why not try a similar activity in the summer with socks on your feet in a paddling pool? Which ones keep your feet driest longest?

What's in it for the children?

This is a really multiple sensory way of playing and exploring materials and in particular their waterproof (or not) characteristics. It is great for encouraging lots of early scientific language.

 Health & Safety

Always supervise children around water.

Growing

What you need:

- Easy care seeds and bedding plants
- A wide variety of containers including Wellington boots, watering cans, old metal jugs etc
- Compost

What to do:

1. With the children plant up boots, jugs, pots etc with plants and seeds and then decorate your outdoor area with them.

2. Encourage children to tend to the plants over time.

Top tip ⭐

Make sure, wherever possible, you put holes in the bottom of containers to aid drainage.

Taking it forward

- Plant up a herb garden in a Wellington boot or growing a wild flower garden in an old tyre.

- Fill a hollow log with compost and plant some trailing plants or even cut the top off an old football and fill it with compost and flowers. Try anything that will grab the children's imagination and make the growing outdoors experience even more exciting.

What's in it for the children?

Growing their own plants and looking after them is a great way for young children to interact first hand with nature and learn abut what things need to grow and where foods come from. Planting in a wide and interesting variety of containers will really engage the children in gardening and encourage them to continue looking after and interacting with the plants. It also helps to make your outdoor area even more exciting and interesting and might help to recycle a few items at the same time!

Bird feeder balls

What you need:

- Some blocks of lard
- A large messy play tray
- Bags of bird seed
- Pine cones
- String

Taking it forward

- Fill yoghurt pots or coconut shells with the mix and hanging up for birds.

- Try squishing some bird seed mix into an open pine cone and hanging out for the birds.

- Make a set of bird spotter cards and make up a bird spotting bag, including books and binoculars, so children can watch to see which birds come to feed on the mix.

What's in it for the children?

Messy play provides children with lots of opportunities to explore the world using their senses. This activity combines a unique messy play experience with the chance to attract wildlife and all of the excitement that bird spotting can bring. Don't forget that while children are squashing and squishing they are developing those all important muscles in hands, wrists and fingers ready for holding pencils in the future.

Top tip ★

Be mindful of cultural issue around using animal fats.

What to do:

1. Allow the lard to reach room temperature. Then break it into chunks and put in the tray.

2. Sprinkle on the bird seed and encourage the children to explore with their hands. Allow lots of squishing and squeezing and exploring with their sense of touch.

3. Encourage children to make the bird seed mix into balls and place in an old satsuma or lemon net from the supermarket and hang somewhere so that the birds can feed on it.

Matchbox challenge

- A selection of small matchboxes

What to do:

1. Challenge the children to fit as many things into their matchbox as they can. Searching around outdoors, children will generally initially just grab anything they can and squash it in. After a while they can be encouraged to search out small objects that will fit in their boxes.

2. When they have all finished searching encourage the children to empty the matchboxes and count how many things they have. Who has the most? Who has the smaller object? The biggest item etc?

Taking it forward

- Encourage children to look for things that start with a specific sound to go in their boxes Can they search out objects which are a particular colour, shape etc.?

- Ask children to suggest and search for their own collections.

What's in it for the children?

This is a lovely small scale activity which gives children first hand experience of small objects and helps to build their size vocabulary. It also encourages lots of exploring and early science investigation as well as access to counting with much larger numbers than they might encounter on a daily basis.

Top tip ★

Try covering the outside of your boxes with sticky-backed plastic to make them last longer.

Cola fountain

What you need:

- Cheap bottle of diet cola (2 litre)
- Small piece of plastic tubing to fit the neck of the bottle or a cardboard tube rolled to fit
- A packet of Mentos mints
- A clear open space
- Head to toe clothing for the adult or children taking part unless you want to come home sticky and covered in cola!

What to do:

1. Stand the cola bottle somewhere outside.
2. Take off the lid.
3. Place a piece of card across the top of the bottle.
4. Place the card or plastic tube on top of the card, so that nothing can fall through the bottom into the cola.
5. Now fill the tube with about half a pack of mints.
6. When you are ready slide the card away so that the mints drop down through the tube into the cola.
7. Get out of the way!
8. Your cola will spray up to 20 feet in the air! A really impressive cola fountain.

Taking it forward

- Try making mini cola fountains with small drink bottles.
- Set up a mixing kitchen and see what concoctions you can make.
- Try adding other things to the cola … what happens? Does something other than cola work?

What's in it for the children?

This is really a 'Wow!' activity to show children that science can be fun and amazing. It shows that mixing things together can have certain effects.

Top tip ⭐

Warm cola makes for higher fountains. Salt or ice added to cola will make it fizz too.

Rainbows in the snow

What you need:

- Spray water bottles
- Squirty bottles
- Coloured paint
- Warm water

Taking it forward

- Try adding some salt to the coloured water mixture. What effect does that have?

- Make snowballs and pile them up and squirt them with your coloured water to make coloured snow sculptures.

- Fill a tough spot tray with ice from the freezer in summer and try squirting coloured waters onto it (snow isn't always a winter activity).

Top tip ⭐

This works best first thing in the morning when snow surfaces are undisturbed.

What to do:

1. On a snowy day fill the bottles with a range of warm coloured water using coloured paints (fluorescent paints are great for this!)

2. Encourage children to squirt rainbows and other designs onto the snow.

3. Talk about what happens when the warm water hits the snow and what happens when you mix two different colours together.

What's in it for the children?

This is a great way of combining materials exploration and provides first hand experience of the elements and creativity. Children get to experience melting first hand as part of a fun exploration of colour.

Light catcher

What you need:

- Old CDs
- String
- Pieces of tin foil,
- Coloured Cellophane
- Sticky tape
- Glitter, foil ribbon and other reflective materials

What to do:

1. Stick two old CDs together so that the silver rainbow side is facing out on both sides. Attach a loop of string to the top of the CDs so you can hang them.

2. Take a piece or pieces of string and attach foil, coloured Cellophane and metallic ribbon. Attach to the bottom of the CD. Hang somewhere where it will catch the sunlight as it turns (a tree or fence is ideal).

Taking it forward

- Stick coloured Cellophane or clear sweet wrappers to a piece of clear sticky-backed plastic and then stick it to a window to allow light to pass through and produce coloured shadows.

- Try hanging pieces of Perspex mirror (shaped versions can be picked up from homeware and DIY stores) to a piece of string and suspending them so that the light is reflected back.

- Attach a glass prism (available from educational suppliers) to a piece of string and hang it up. It will produce a rainbow on the floor when the light catches it. Try using glass beads from an old lampshade or chandelier.

- Drape your outdoor den making area with some sequined material. It will catch the sunlight and produce lovely patterns as children play.

What's in it for the children?

Through this creative activity children are able to explore both light and colour as they go about their ongoing outdoor play. This activity is really about helping the children to enhance their learning environment and to make it even more engaging for them to explore.

Wind trailers

What you need:

- A selection of wooden curtain rings
- A selection of hair scrunchies
- A wide selection of ribbons in different colours, lengths, widths and materials

What to do:

1. Tie a variety of different ribbons to a curtain ring and allow children to run round and explore the way the ribbons trail in the wind.

Taking it forward

- Try attaching ribbons to the outside of a hoopla hoop and hang it up horizontally to blow in the wind or let the children run around with it as a big wind trailer.

- Tie a range of ribbons of different lengths to sticks and stand them in the ground to blow in the wind. Can you tell which way the wind is blowing?

What's in it for the children?

An important part of outdoor learning is to be prepared to respond to the weather conditions as and when they change. Having a selection of wind trailers will help children to really engage with the weather on windy days and get really active on calm sunny days.

Top tip ★

Try tying the ribbons to a scrunchy instead and children can wear them on their wrists and run around.

Nature sun prints

What you need:

- **Sun print paper** (available online **www.amazon.co.uk**)
- **A selection of leaves and other natural materials with interesting shapes** (ferns make nice shapes)
- **Water** (see instructions for sealing prints)

What to do:

1. Follow the instructions on the sun print paper. You will have to lay objects on your paper, expose to sunlight and then fix the prints (usually by dipping the paper in water).

2. Exposure to the sun quickly changes the colour of the paper leaving a shadow of the shape on the paper in a darker colour.

Taking it forward

- Lay out brightly coloured sugar paper in the sun, place objects onto the paper and leave for a few hours until the paper fades. Can you see the shapes? Try doing this on a big scale with large objects such as wheels, balls and even bicycle wheels.

What's in it for the children?

This is a fun science activity with shows children a really quick change (reaction) in the paper and combines early science understanding with creativity. It has that instant 'Wow!' factor that gets young children really excited about science and finding out about the world.

Cup pyramid

What you need:

- A selection of clear plastic cups
- Water
- Jugs
- Food colouring

What to do:

1. Glue the cups together with strong glue to form a cup pyramid with the cups facing upwards (see picture). Stand the tower on a shallow tray to allow water to collect at the bottom.

2. Provide a wide range of different coloured water and encourage children to pour it into different parts of the tower until it starts to overflow into the next cup down. Can they get the water to flow from the top to the bottom? What happens when they pour two different colours at the same time?

Taking it forward

- Make smaller cup towers with plastic shot glasses or bigger ones with plastic flower buckets.

What's in it for the children?

Children need lots of opportunities to revisit their understanding and experiences in a range of different ways. This activity encourages children to have fun pouring water outdoors in a situation other than the standard water tray, at the same time as exploring the way the water behaves as they pour it. It also provides a fun colour-mixing activity.

Icy paint slopes

What you need:

- Paints and or food colouring
- Ice cube trays
- Piece of wood and bricks or crates to make a slope
- Paper to cover the slope.

What to do:

1. Make up coloured ice cubes by adding paint or food colouring to water.

2. Set up a slope and cover it with a piece of paper (clip it to the top so it doesn't move).

3. Take some coloured ice cubes and place them at the top of the slope and let them go. As they slide down the slope talk about the way that the melting ice leaves coloured trails on the paper. Try with other colours. Which ones move best? Can children get them to slide faster? Slower?

4. Once you have a rainbow trail on the paper you can take it off and dry it. Try again with the cubes that are melting now, does it make a difference to the colour?

Taking it forward

- Try making some big coloured bricks in the same way, but in larger plastic containers and see how they go down your slope. Try making a big scale slope to slide the giant cubes down.

What's in it for the children?

This a lovely combination of creativity, colour exploration and playing with forces and the effects of gravity. As children play with different slopes they will explore cause and effect first hand.

Top tip ⭐

You can freeze neat poster paint for really bright colours.

Bubble stream

What you need:

- **Used, clean soda bottles** (both 2 litre and smaller ones)
- **Pieces of flannel**
- **Some elastic bands**
- **Bubble mixture and water**
- **Scissors**

SKIN allergy !

What to do:

1. Cut the bottom off the bottle.
2. Attach a piece of flannel over the bottom of the cut off bottle using an elastic band.
3. Dip the flannel end into the bubble mixture until it is soaked.
4. Blow through the neck end of the bottle and watch as lots and lots of bubbles start to appear from the end of your bubble tube. How long can you make your bubble stream?

Taking it forward

- Try making smaller bubble blowers with small drinks bottles.
- Have a go at making your own bubble mixtures with other materials: explore bubble bath, toothpaste, shower gel, shaving foam, washing-up liquid etc to see which makes the most or the best bubbles.

What's in it for the children?

This is a great way for children to play and explore bubble making in a unique way. It encourages lots of language around the amount of bubbles or the biggest bubble or the longest stream of bubbles.

Top tip ★

For hygiene reasons make sure bubble bottles are labelled with children's names and they only use their own bottles to blow in to minimise contamination. Wash all bottles well after use.

Bug dipping

What you need:

- **Some fishing nets** (the type used to go rock pooling on the beach)
- **A white sheet**
- **A selection of magnifiers and magnifying glasses**

What to do:

1. Take the nets and find a piece of overgrown hedgerow. Encourage the children to sweep the nets over the hedgerow, making sure to dip into the grasses and flowers.

2. When everyone has 'bug dipped' take the nets and empty them onto a large white sheet. That way any small creatures and minibeasts will show up no matter what size or colour. Ask questions such as 'What did you manage to find? Can you take photographs of your finds? How many legs do they have? What colour are they?'

3. Use magnifiers and magnifying glasses to look closer at your finds. Return any creatures to their natural habitat afterwards.

Top tip ⭐

This activity works best in late spring and early summer when there are lots of minibeasts in the hedgerows.

Taking it forward

- Try bug dipping at different times of the year and in different places. Do you find different things?

- Can you find minibeasts anywhere else in your outdoor area? Try looking under logs and stones?

What's in it for the children?

This is a great way of collecting and discovering minibeasts in the children's own surroundings and is a fun way of exploring their own world at different times of year.

Bird seed pictures in winter

FOOD allergy!

What you need:

- A selection of different bird seed in a wide variety of colours
- A snowy or a frosty surface

What to do:

1. On a snow covered surface encourage children to make pictures with the different coloured bird seed. Once they have explored the different shapes and sizes talk with the children about which birds might eat the food and why they might need it on cold days

2. Leave the seed designs for a few hours or overnight and see what the birds eat. If you are really quiet you may be able to see the birds visiting and try and identify which types of birds they are.

> ### Top tip
> Contrasting colours stand out best in snow.

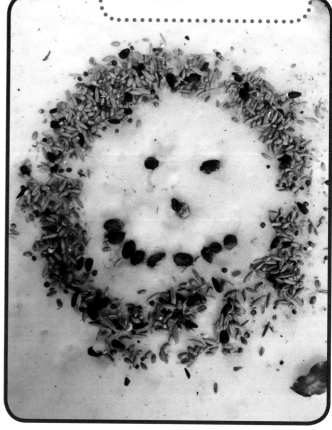

Taking it forward

- Try making bird feeder balls (page 19) to try and attract birds to your outdoor setting.

- Make pictures with other seeds or nuts (be aware of allergies).

What's in it for the children?

This is a great way of encouraging wildlife into your outdoor area so children can experience them first hand. Putting food out in cold weather also helps in building understanding of why birds and other animals need food to stay healthy. At the same time the activity allows children to be creative and explore lots of seeds and grains.

Build an insect hotel

What you need:

- Three wooden pallets
- Old roof tiles
- Pieces of drain pipe
- Straw, dry leaves and twigs
- Bamboo canes cut into small lengths

What to do:

1. Stack the pallets on top of each other in an area away from your main play area which insects can access without being disturbed.

2. Stuff the gaps in the pallets with the other materials, being sure to make lots of small holes and gaps for small insects to crawl into.

3. Building an insect hotel will encourage a wide range of insects and creatures to start living in your outdoor space and as warmer weather sets in these creatures will then readily explore your garden for food and nectar. Encourage children to look for and identify insects when they see them. (See also *The Little Book of Minibeast Hotels* by Ann Roberts (Featherstone))

Taking it forward

- Try making up some spotter bags (children's garden tool bags available online stuffed with pads, pencils, magnifiers and bug spotter cards or books). Visit **www.naturedetectives.co.uk** for lots of downloadable spotter cards for every season.

- Plant flowers that attract insects to your setting. Buddleia and lavender are easy to grow favourites for insects and butterflies.

What's in it for the children?

Attracting insects and wildlife to your outdoor area gives children the chance to explore the living world first hand rather than through books or on a computer. The more living things you can attract to your outdoor area the more children will understand the complex interactions that take place in the natural world.

Water beads

What you need:

- **Clear water beads** (available online)
- **A water tray**
- **Water**
- **Fishing nets** (the kind used in fish tanks, available from pet stores and supermarkets)

Taking it forward

- Try using coloured water beads as part of your ongoing water play.
- Explore water beads in other materials other than water. Try sand or shaving foam.

What's in it for the children?

This is a lovely, unusual activity for encouraging children to explore with their sense of touch as well as sight. It leads to lots of talking and development of early science language such as squishy, wet, slimey etc. Remember children can really develop their sensory awareness as part of everyday play.

 Health & Safety

Clear away any broken beads immediately and make sure you supervise at all times to avoid any choking hazards.

What to do:

1. Follow the manufacturer's instructions to hydrate the water beads (usually soak overnight).

2. Place your water beads in a tray of water. Once in the water you will not be able to see the beads.

3. Encourage the children to initially explore the water tray with their hands. What can they feel? What can they find? Using the nets, how many beads can you catch?

4. Encourage children to play with and explore the beads with cups and scoops as part of their play.

puddle painting

What you need:

- **Powder paint in a variety of colours.**
- **Brushes: lots of different sizes including washing-up brushes and toilet brushes** (new of course!)
- **Large sheets of white paper**
- **Puddles: either occurring naturally or make your own on a sunny day**

Taking it forward

- Try mixing on a large scale in puddles by shaking on powder paint and using mops and brooms to mix and move the puddles around.

- Use marbling inks in your puddle instead of powder paints and see what patterns you can make. Use paper to lift off the marbling ink pattern.

- Add washing-up liquid and make bubbles in your puddle paintings. Lay paper over to take a bubble print.

- Use fluorescent powder paint and lay on black paper to take the print.

What's in it for the children?

This is a truly multi-sensory way of exploring children's direct environment and developing their natural curiosity as well as their creativity. It provides a lovely way of experiencing first hand how materials change as you play with them.

What to do:

1. Encourage children to explore the puddles by shaking the powder paints onto the surface of the puddles and mixing with the brushes. What colours can you make?

2. Try laying a piece of paper on top of the puddle and lifting off a print.

Top tip ⭐

Use a selection of old glitter shakers or salt shakers to dispense the coloured powder paint.

Dancing on ice

What you need:

- A selection of small figures
- Ice cube trays
- Access to a freezer
- A builder's tray or flat table top

Taking it forward

- If the weather is really cold you could try adding a small amount of water to the builder's tray and leaving out overnight to freeze and form an ice rink for your ice characters to skate on.

- Make some big skaters by freezing the feet of larger toys into larger tubs of ice.

- Make coloured ice marbles (ball ice cube makers are available online). Roll them across a tray: What happens when they hit each other?

What's in it for the children?

This activity not only encourages children to play with and explore the properties of ice as they play, including how it feels and behaves, but also is a great way of exploring simple forces as the children push the skaters across the ice.

Top tip ⭐

If you are having difficulty getting the figures to skate well, add a little water to the surface of the tray.

What to do:

1. Partially fill the ice cube trays and freeze.

2. Take out of the freezer and stand the figure in the middle of each ice cube. Add more water and refreeze so that the figures feet are frozen into the cubes.

3. Take the cubes out and add to a builder's tray. Explore getting the characters to dance on the ice by pushing them. Can the children get the figures to do spins? Which one goes the furthest? Which one goes the fastest? What happens if one skater crashes into another? What happens as the ice starts to melt?

Clattering things

What you need:

- **A wide selection of pots, pans and bowls made of different materials** (metal, plastic, wood etc)
- **A selection of spoons made from wood, plastic and metal**

What to do:

1. Encourage children to freely explore how they can make sounds using the various pots and pans. Talk about how to make sounds louder, softer, quieter. Which materials make the best sound? What happens if your change your spoon beater? Does it change the sound?

2. Encourage children to explore around their outdoor environment to see if they can make other noises with their tools.

Taking it forward

- Try hanging the pots and pans from a fence or shed wall so children can explore this as a 'music wall'.

- Put different metal bowls in the water tray and try hitting them with metal spoons to make sounds.

What's in it for the children?

The outdoor environment gives children the chance to explore sound at a much louder level than is usually practical indoors. Giving children lots of opportunity to explore making sounds outdoors not only encourages creativity and expression but builds on their understanding of materials and their properties. Be sure to make some kind of sound exploration available at all times.

Ball roll painting

What you need:

- A small blow-up paddling pool or a plastic play tray
- Large sheets of paper to cover the bottom of the pool
- A selection of ready made paint in a variety of colours
- A selection of different types of balls in different sizes.

What to do:

1. Cover the bottom of the paddling pool with paper (stick it down with masking tape if necessary).

2. Pour some blobs of paint onto the paper in different places.

3. Place some of the balls (two or three) into the pool.

4. Encourage a small group of children to lift up the pool together and work together to tilt the pool and make the balls roll through the paint. Which ball rolls fastest? How can we make it roll faster? Which ball makes the best pattern?

5. Encourage children to continue exploring the process with other balls of different sizes from small marbles to large basket balls. Does the size affect the way the balls roll?

Taking it forward

- Use lots of natural materials to roll around in the paint. Try conkers, pebbles, pine cones, acorns etc.

- Set up small individual trays lined with paper (seed trays work well) so that children can individually explore rolling materials.

- Try rolling objects across large pieces of paper on the ground.

What's in it for the children?

This is a really fun and creative way of exploring how objects move and how we can influence how they move. It also encourages lots of co-operative play and problem solving and is great as an adult-initiated but child-led exploration.

Rain painting

What you need:

- **Shallow trays** (unused cat litter or seed trays are ideal)
- **Paper**
- **Powder paint in a variety of colours**

What to do:

1. This is an activity to do if you know it is about to rain or if you are thinking of going out for some time on a rainy day.

2. Cover the base of the trays with paper.

3. Sprinkle a variety of colours of powder paint onto the paper.

4. Take the trays out and wait for the rain to help you make a paint pattern.

5. When you are happy with your rain painting, take it undercover to dry.

Taking it forward

- Try this on a large scale by taping a huge piece of paper to the ground outdoors (wallpaper lining is a cheap way of doing large scale paper activities). Shake powder paints across the paper and wait for the rain to give you a helping hand.

- Try adding glitter to your powder paint for added sparkle.

What's in it for the children?

This is a great way of combining observation and interaction with the weather and creativity. While the rain mixes to make the paintings, children also get first had experience of colour mixing and how materials change.

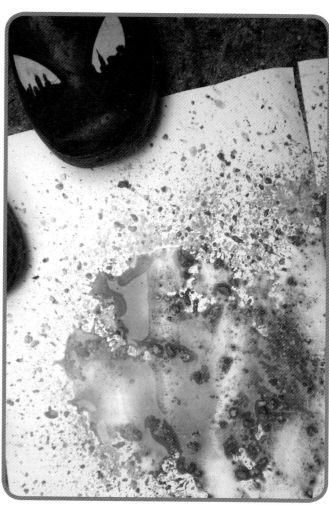

Top tip ⭐

Use sugar or flour shakers to easily dispense powder paints.

Build a big scale nest

What you need:

- A wide selection of sticks, twigs, leaves, feathers and other materials used for nest building, as large as you can find

What to do:

1. The idea behind this activity is to engage children with the process of how birds build nests, not by creating a small version with a few bits of twig, but by building a nest scaled to the children.

2. Talk with children about nests, discuss who builds nests and why. Look at pictures of nests and try to see what materials have been used to build them.

3. Challenge the children to build their own nest. Encourage them to think about how big they are and how big the nest needs to be. Encourage problem solving such as 'Which sticks bend best?', 'How do you get the twigs and sticks to stick together?', 'How can you make the nest comfortable?'.

Taking it forward

- Why not make some giant papier mâché eggs (using balloons covered in paper and PVA glue) and encourage role play with the eggs in the nest?

- Put up a bird box and see if you can encourage a bird to really nest in or near to your setting.

What's in it for the children?

This is great not only for exploring the process of nature but because it provides lots of opportunities to solve problems and to work collaboratively to solve the children's own questions. It links science and nature really nicely with outdoor role play once the nest is built as children can revisit their nest for play opportunities.

What you need:

- Lengths of foil air duct tubing (available from DIY stores)
- A wide selection of different sized play cars

Taking it forward

- Cut up the tubing into different lengths and explore with the cars.

- Explore what else you can roll down the tubes. Does it make different sounds? Does it go faster than the cars? (Try tennis balls, marbles, pine cones, pebbles etc.).

What's in it for the children?

This offers the chance for children to explore the way the cars move through the tubing, and to set up their own experiments to adjust speed and sound. They can work together in co-operative play and problem solving.

Top tip ⭐

Put some masking tape or electrical tape around the rim of the tubing to stop any potential scratching. The tubing is quite easily flattened, so if this happens just chop off the flattened bit and start again!

What to do:

1. Offer the tubing stretched out with small cars as an invitation to play outdoors.

2. Encourage children to explore what happens when they put a car in one end of the tube. Will it come out the other end? How can they help it?

3. Notice how the cars make a noise as they run through the tubing. Can you get the car to make a louder, quieter, longer, noise? What happens when you put a smaller or a larger car in the tube?

4. The tubing is pliable so the children can also explore bends and bumps in the tubing.

Nature crowns

What you need:

- Long strips of card
- Double sided sticky tape
- Stapler

What to do:

1. Stick a strip of double sided tape to the card strip and fit to a child's head and staple to make a fitted crown which is sticky on the outside. Repeat to make a crown for every child in the group.

2. Either encourage children to explore the immediate outdoor environment or go for a walk and collect natural objects as you go. Each time they find something they can stick it to their crown to create a nature crown. When they return you can have look at and talk about all of the things they have found.

Taking it forward

- In autumn go on a leaf hunt and make leaf crowns with different shapes and colours.

- Try making a colour crown, looking for natural objects that are all the same colour or try making a rainbow of natural materials on your crown.

- Once you have explored the skills of making nature crowns you can leave a supply of materials available outdoors at all times so that children can access them when they wish.

- Put out a huge sheet of sticky-backed plastic, sticky side up and work together as a group to find and collect different natural objects and stick them to your sheet. When you have finished you can stick the plastic to a window pane.

What's in it for the children?

This activity allows individual children to make their own collection of objects without the need for bags or pockets. As well as encouraging children to look at and explore the natural world more closely, it offers elements of creativity as well.

Chalk drawing

What you need:

- A selection of coloured chalks
- Sandpaper
- Zip food bags
- Water
- Pots
- Paintbrushes
- Cotton wool
- A mallet or hammer

What to do:

Wet chalk

1. Dip one end of a piece of chalk into a small bowl of water and leave for about ten minutes until the chalk is soaked through.

2. Explore drawing on the pavement, walls, or wood stumps. Are there differences in colour, texture etc from dry chalk (wet chalk makes colours much more vibrant)?

3. Try mixing two colours together.

Chalk dust

1. Put some coloured chalk in a freezer bag and seal (making sure to squeeze out excess air). Now crush the chalk to a dust using the hammer or mallet. The bag ensures the dust doesn't go everywhere.

2. When in powder form, tip out into a dish and encourage children to explore making patterns with the coloured dust. Use cotton wool balls and dry paintbrushes to make patterns.

3. Alternatively try rubbing coloured chalk on to sandpaper to make your chalk dust.

Chalk paint

1. Take your coloured chalk dust and add water a little at a time and stir until you have a paste-like consistency. Now explore painting onto pavements, bricks, wooden blocks etc with your coloured chalk paint. What happens when the paint dries? Does the colour change? What happens if you add water again?

Taking it forward

- Try crushing or sandpapering two or more coloured chalks together. What colours can you make?

- Add coloured chalk dust to your mud kitchen to make coloured mud pies etc.

- Add other liquids to your chalk dust: washing-up liquid, toothpaste etc and explore mixing

What's in it for the children?

This is just a great way of exploring the same material in lots of different ways as part of creative play outdoors. Children are able to explore first hand lots of textures and mixing colours too.

Science laboratory

What you need:

- **Lots of plastic tubes similar to test tubes** (you can buy these online or collect old glitter tubes)
- **Selection of jugs, cups, water syringes, droppers, spoons, stirrers, turkey boasters etc.**
- **White vinegar**
- **Water**
- **Bicarbonate of soda** (available from baking aisle in supermarkets)
- **Lemon juice**
- **Food colouring**
- **Some old white adult shirts**
- **DIY plastic safety goggles** (available from pound shops)

What to do:

1. Set up your mixing laboratory with a wide selection of mixing instruments, containers etc.
2. Let the children put on their lab coats (old shirt) and their safety goggles.
3. Colour lots of water, white vinegar and lemon juice with different food colours.
4. Encourage children to explore mixing with the different coloured liquids and powders. Can they make a frothy mixture?

Top tip ★

Why not try linking this activity to the story of **George's Marvellous Medicine** by Roald Dahl or **Charlie and the Chocolate Factory** by Roald Dahl for extra excitement.

Taking it forward

- Over a period of time introduce lots of different materials to your mixing lab. Try adding lemonade, ice, glitter, dry tapioca (it swells up when wet), rice, flour, cornflour, toothpaste, shaving foam etc.

What's in it for the children?

This is a really great multi-sensory play experience which allows children to experiment, try things out, change their minds, make discoveries and draw conclusions all as part of play. This is great for encouraging lots of talking and communicating of ideas as well as problem solving.

squishy feet: sensory trays

What you need:

- **A selection of shallow trays** (boot trays or cat litter trays are ideal and available cheaply)
- **A selection of natural materials with different textures such as squishy mud, cut grass, crunchy leaves, sand** (dry and very wet) **gravel, etc**

What to do:

1. Encourage the children to explore the trays with their bare feet by standing in them with the natural materials inside. Promote lots of talk about how it feels and the sounds that they hear as they stand in the tray: squishy, crunchy, sharp, smooth, slushy are all good words.

2. Which tray is your favourite? Which one do you like least? Which one can you make the best noise in? Which one can you make the loudest noise in?

3. By offering lots of open ended questions children can explore their sense of touch with their feet and find their own answers to questions.

Taking it forward

- Retell stories such as *We're Going on a Bear Hunt* by Michael Rosen (Walker) using the tray to tell it. Make a snowy tray by scraping ice from the freezer or using instant snow powder (available online) which stays cold to the touch. Encourage children to suggest what can be used for the 'stumble trip' tray or the 'squelch squelch' one?

- Try adding other materials to the trays for children to explore: wet sawdust, sand with washing-up liquid and water (sand mousse), cooked tapioca, etc.

- Add mud and water to a small blow-up padding pool or builder's tray and encourage children to explore it with their whole bodies. Nothing beats getting hands and feet in squelchy mud – make sure you have washing facilities at hand and changes of clothes!

Top tip ⭐

Have towels and warm soapy water available so the children can wash their feet. Supervise them at all times to avoid slipping hazards.

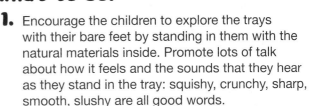

What's in it for the children?

As well as providing an unusual way of exploring the sense of touch, this activity is great for finding out about children's own individual likes and dislikes and hence good for combining early science with emotional development. When used to retell stories it can act as a powerful tool for developing language and talking skills.

Scented soup making

What you need:

- Either a small blow-up paddling pool or a selection of large plastic mixing bowls.
- Large wooden spoons (you can buy spoons up to 1 metre long online see **www.mindstretchers. co.uk**)
- Water
- A selection of herbs and scented plants (lavender, curry plant, basil, parsley, rosemary, chives, lemon thyme, mint etc: preferably for children to select their own from plants grown in your garden, otherwise these are all widely available from supermarkets and garden centres)
- Scissors
- Soup related stories: **Pumpkin Soup or Delicious!** by Helen Cooper (Corgi Children's Books), **Stone Soup** by Heather Forest (August House Publishers) or **Dragon Soup** by Michael Yu (Children's ebook).

What to do:

1. Explore soup based stories with the children and discuss what they might want to put in their own 'soup'.

2. Encourage the children to explore creating their own soup by putting water (coloured is even more exciting) into the paddling pool or bowls and adding scented ingredients . As children chose ingredients encourage them to explore using their sense of smell and touch.

3. Encourage role play by providing small bowls and ladles for serving your soup.

Top tip ⭐

As with all food explorations be mindful of food allergies and wash hands thoroughly after play.

Taking it forward

- Offer other ingredients to add to soups. Try scented dried herbs such as cinnamon, star anise, cloves, turmeric etc. (don't use any form of pepper or chillies as these can be irritating to skin and eyes.

- Have available jars and pots so children can bottle and maybe even sell their soup creations.

What's in it for the children?

This is a really lovely way of combining imaginative story telling and role play with exploration of our senses. It is much more fun than a few yoghurt pots filled with different smelly things! Children gain a real insight into different smells and the science language such as smell, sweet, spicy etc related to smell, while keeping it firmly within their own play experiences.

Home-made metal detector

What you need:

- Magnet wands and/or large horseshoe magnets
- A selection of metal and non metal objects: tin cans, jar lids, paper clips, nuts and bolts, spoons, coins etc
- A sand tray or pit
- A laminated list of the metallic objects you want the children to find.
- Baskets for collecting items
- Dry wipe markers

What to do:

1. Photograph and laminate pictures of the metallic objects you have selected (make sure to use a wide selection of different sizes).

2. Bury your objects in the sand.

3. Give children their treasure hunting lists and their metal detectors (you can cover the handles of the magnet wands with tin foil to make them look more exciting).

4. Encourage children to move the detectors around in the sand and see if they can find the objects. Encourage talk about the objects which they find that won't stick to the metal detector. Do they have ideas about why not?

5. Try adding pirate costumes to enhance the treasure hunt play experience or treasure hunter hats (like Indiana Jones!).

Taking it forward

- Take your metal detectors around the outdoor setting and see if you can find any other metal objects.

- Make a magnetic sensory tray by placing lots of metallic objects in a cat litter or seed tray and leaving it with magnets for children to explore freely. This is a nice activity for doing on a lawn in sunny weather.

- Try using bought metal detectors to find things in your sand area. See www.tts-group. co.uk

What's in it for the children?

This is a fun way of exploring materials and magnetism within the context of children's play. Making science a part of role play makes it much more engaging for young children.

Top tip ★

Wrap the end of your wands or magnets in a bit of cling film to protect them from getting scratched by the sand.

Pendulum play

What you need:

- **String**
- **Bamboo canes**
- **Paper** (large sheets are best)
- **Plastic cups**
- **Watered down poster paints** in a variety of colours

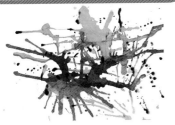

Taking it forward

- You can have a go at trying this activity on a really big scale by using a bucket or an old paint tin with a handle and a hole in the bottom and swinging over a really big piece of paper.

What's in it for the children?

This is a really creative hands-on way of exploring forces and how our actions affect how things move. This is a good example of large scale creativity combined with early science.

Top tip ⭐

Try using an old plastic squirty sauce bottle (the type you get in cafés and for barbecues) cut the bottom off the bottle and string up as with the cup. Allow the paint to drizzle out through the nozzle.

What to do:

1. Construct a basic framework with the canes and the string either by lashing them together in a teepee formation or by hanging a can from two canes pushed into the ground.

2. Make three or four holes in the top lip of the cup and tie string through. Attach the ends of the string to the framework or pole so that the cup sits straight and is able to swing freely.

3. Push a hole in the base of the cup and then place a piece of masking tape over it.

4. Pour some watered-down paint into the cup.

5. Carefully remove the tape so that the paint begins to drip/pour through onto the paper.

6. Now push the cup so that it swings like a pendulum making a great pattern on the paper.

7. Once the paint runs out you can add different colours and try again. What happens if you swing the cup harder or in a different direction?

Mud and clay painting

What you need:

- Mud
- Clay
- Water
- Paint
- Pots
- Paintbrushes

What to do:

1. Mix up some mud paints by putting a small amount of mud into a pot or jar. Jars are better as you can see the different colours through them, although clear plastic cups work well and don't break as easily.

2. Gradually add water and mix to a paste-like consistency. Make different coloured paints by mixing together with paint. Try different types of soil and mud and adding things like chalk.

3. You can create a nice white paint by crushing up chalk (directly from the ground is ideal but shop-bought works well too), adding water as before and mixing.

4. Crushed up bricks make a great red-based paint and clay mixed with water gives a lovely textured brown or orange paint.

5. Encourage children to explore painting with their earth paints on pebbles, log slices and on the ground or on paper.

Taking it forward

- Dig holes in the ground and make your paints in natural dug out paint pots which can be filled in when they are finished with.

- Try looking at some aboriginal artwork and offer mud paints with cotton buds to see if children can make their own tribal patterns on rocks and wood.

What's in it for the children?

This activity gives children the chance to explore textures and materials first hand while being creative. As the paints dry they can observe the changes.

Muddy puddles

 Health & Safety

Always supervise children around open water. When not in use cover with a tarpaulin to prevent children falling in.

What you need:

- A muddy digging area
- Water
- A selection of natural objects including pine cones, sticks, feathers etc
- Children with Wellington boots and waterproofs

What to do:

1. Dig the soil over and add water until you have a really big muddy puddle. Encourage the children to explore jumping and splashing in the mud and the water. Promote language to describe the sounds and the feel of the mud: squelchy, squishy, soggy, etc.

2. Try adding some of the natural materials to the water and seeing what happens. Do they float? Don't make this a tedious 'one object in one out' task but allow the children to explore the materials themselves in the water together. What is the heaviest thing they can put in which floats?

Taking it forward

- Use bigger logs or stones. What if you try shells? (Some will float to start with and then sink as they fill with water.)
- Make wooden rafts with twigs (see page 6) and float them in your puddle.
- Try making ice boats ice with sticks frozen in and paper sails added afterwards.

What's in it for the children?

For so many children their only exploration of the concept of floating and sinking is in a water tray. This activity allows children to explore water with their whole bodies and play with a wide range of natural materials as they explore what happens to them.

Top tip

Let water soak into the mud for a while, once the mud is waterlogged it will get stickier and your puddle will stay for longer and you can have much more fun!

Tin can walkie talkies

What you need:

- **Two tin cans** (empty and washed, with sharp edges filed or covered with electrical tape)
- **String** (about 3 metres)
- **Scissors**
- **A screwdriver or bradawl**

What to do:

1. Make a hole in the bottom of both tin cans with the bradawl or the screwdriver.

2. Thread the string through the hole and knot on the inside of the tin.

3. Thread the remaining end of the string through the inside of the second can and knot again on the inside of the tin.

4. Go outside and encourage the children to stand with the string tight and for one child to talk into one can while the other holds the second can to their ear. Can they hear their friends?

5. What happens if the string isn't tight?

Taking it forward

- Send each other messages through the string. Can your friend make out what you said?

- Try sending the name of an object through the string and see if your friend can find the object for you.

- Talk through other things like pieces of drain pipe or plastic tubing. Try metal air ducting tubing from a DIY store.

What's in it for the children?

This is a really fun way of encouraging children to develop their sense of hearing and to explore sounds as part of their play. It makes use of the extra space available outdoors as it encourages children to develop their speaking and listening skills as well as their early science understanding.

Top tip ⭐

If you can't use tin cans use polystyrene cups — they work well too.

Floating fruit

What you need:

- A selection of fruits and vegetables including pumpkins of different sizes, melons, satsumas, pears, apples etc.
- A water tray

What to do:

1. Fill the water tray and encourage children to explore putting the fruit and veg into it. What happens? (Apples float, some pears sink.) Do all the heavy things sink?

2. What happens if you cut up the fruit (adult task). What happens if you peel some of the fruit? (Sometimes satsumas and oranges will float with skins on and sink or partially sink with them peeled off!)

Taking it forward

- Try filling a paddling pool with water, giving children really big wooden spoons (you can get 1 metre spoons online) and encourage them to make 'soup' by stirring in different vegetables, fruit and other things that they find around the outdoor setting. Link with a story like *Delicious!* by Helen Cooper (Corgi Children's Books) for added literacy and language fun.

- Encourage children to explore lots of heavier items in their water play: Do they all sink? Try a really big candle or a piece of pumice stone.

What's in it for the children?

Part of early science is for children to build on their existing understanding and to be challenged. This is not about you saying 'No that's not right' when they offer their theory about why something happens but for you to offer extensions to the activity to take that understanding forward and to challenge their thinking. This activity challenges the often held misconception that things sink because they are heavy.

Top tip ⭐

Try and make the water deep enough so the larger items have enough water to float in.

Nature collection cubes

What you need:

- A large cardboard box
- Scissors
- **Five sheets of clear sticky-backed plastic** (four the same size as the sides of the box and one the same size as the top)

Taking it forward

- Either hang the window cube from a tree or fence to allow children to observe the light passing through it, or place a small battery powered torch or light inside and see what it looks like lit up.
- Give children smaller squares of sticky-backed plastic to make individual collections.
- Encourage children to have a closer look at their finds using magnifiers.

What's in it for the children?

This activity gets children really exploring their outdoor environment and bringing back their finds to discuss and observe further. It is good for encouraging children to work together at the same time as allowing for individual collections of materials.

Top tip ⭐

An extra strip of sticky tape around the sticky-backed plastic helps to make sure it doesn't cave in on over enthusiastic children!

What to do:

1. Cut out the majority of each side of the box leaving a 5 cm frame around the outside. Do the same with the top of the box (leave the bottom whole).

2. Peel the paper off the sticky-backed plastic and stick it to the inside of the sides of the box so that the sticky surface faces out. You should end up with a cube-like structure with sticky windows.

3. Encourage children to collect lots of natural objects from around the setting, advise them to try to keep what they collect quite small. They can then stick what they find to one of the windows. How many colours, shapes etc can they find? Why not stick objects of each colour onto a different window, or let children have a window each to collect their objects?

Make your own pond

What you need:

- **An old water tray or oak barrel** (line with plastic pod liner or tarpaulin)
- **A selection of pond plants from the garden centre**
- **Stones**
- **Water**

What to do:

1. Many settings would love a large pond for children to observe wildlife throughout the year but sadly funds and or space often prevent this being possible. This activity shows that even in the smallest outdoor area you can create a small pond with all the learning possibility of a larger one.

2. Place rocks around the edge of the tray/barrel so that they form a platform for any small wildlife to climb out and to form a ledge for plants which may like shallow water. Arrange your plants around the edges and fill your container with water (preferably rain water as it has less chance of having chemicals in).

3. Leave your pond to settle, this can take a couple of weeks. Wait for the water to go clear and any sediment to settle at the bottom of the tray.

4. Over time, wildlife will be attracted to your pond as it establishes itself. If you add frogspawn from another source remember that young frogs need a way of getting out of the pond or they will drown. They will try to return each year so make sure you are intending your pond to stay where it is for a long time. Ideally any tadpoles/frogs should be returned to the place from which they were sourced.

Top tip ⭐

Try placing a squeezable ball on the surface of your pond in cold weather to enable you to break a hole in the surface of any ice to allow oxygen into the water for wildlife.

Taking it forward

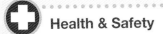 Keep an observation basket near to your pond and encourage children to look closely at what is in the water. Include magnifiers and spotter books. You could even have a selection of dipping nets so they can have a closer look.

What's in it for the children?

Giving children the chance to observe pond life first hand puts their understanding of wildlife and ecology firmly within their own sphere of reference. Children are able to experience first hand the effects of changing seasons on plants and animals as well as observing life cycles in a more natural setting than a plastic tank on a table indoors.

✚ Health & Safety

Remember to supervise children around water to minimise the risk of falling in (a wire net over the top may provide a safer solution for times when you are not working directly with your pond).

Solar powered water play

What you need:

- **A solar powered pond fountain pump kit** (available reasonably cheaply online)

- **A shallow tray of water or a water tray on the floor so children can sit next to the water**

- **Some water** (you can colour the water with food colouring for added interest)

What to do:

1. Follow the instructions to assemble the pump. Place the fountain part into the water and make sure that the solar panel is accessible to the children. Switch on the pump.

2. Encourage children to explore as the water comes up out of the fountain.

3. Show how when you put a hand over the solar panel the pump stops. Let the children try investigating the panel. Invite lots of discussion about how and why it all works. Try using the pump on a really sunny day for the most dramatic effects.

Taking it forward

- If you can afford more than one pump you can have them all working together with a different spray head on each. Or alternatively, change the heads on your pump for differing sprinkle effects.

- Explore other solar powered garden equipment including lights and toys (easily available from pound stores in spring and summer).

- Try adding a mirror or some tin foil to the bottom of your tray to see extra reflections.

What's in it for the children?

This is a lovely way for children to explore cause and effect as well as an early introduction to the idea of solar power. It is the ideal combination of science, technology and water play.

Water music making

What you need:

- A water tray
- Water
- A wide selection of metal bowls and containers (balti dishes, chutney trays etc are easily obtainable from pound like stores)
- Some metal forks and spoons

What to do:

1. Fill the water tray outside.
2. Float the metal dishes and containers in the water.
3. Encourage children to explore hitting the bowls with their spoons and forks to make their own water music. Do the bigger bowls make different sounds to the smaller ones?

Taking it forward

- Try pouring some water into the bowls and hitting again, does it change the sound?
- Use other things to hit the bowls. Try wooden spoons or sticks, plastic spoons etc

What's in it for the children?

This is a great way of exploring sounds as part of a fun water play activity. It is a lovely multi-sensory exploration and leads to lots of language and talk about what children can hear and how they can change the sounds.

Health & Safety

Always supervise children around water.

Ice anchors away

What you need:

- A selection of plastic containers with lids (butter and cottage cheese containers are ideal)
- Water
- Food colouring
- Twigs
- Paper

What to do:

1. Pour a small amount of water into the bottom of the container (about four to five centimetres), add food colouring if you wish at this point.

2. Pierce a hole in the lid of the container in the centre.

3. Push a small twig or stick through the hole in the lid.

4. Place the lid back on the container so that the stick reaches the bottom of the container and sticks up through the lid.

5. Place the container in the fridge and freeze.

6. When frozen remove the lid carefully and then take the 'ice boat' out of the container.

7. Add a paper sail to the stick mast.

8. Encourage children to explore playing with the ice boats in the water tray.

9. What happens as the ice melts?

50 fantastic ideas for science outdoors

Taking it forward

- Try making some ice boats of different sizes, using ice cream containers or take away tubs. Does the size/weight of the boats make a difference to how they behave in the water?

- Use warm water to float your boats in: what difference does it make?

- Make boats from other materials such as tin foil, plastic, empty orange halves etc.

- Have a boat race across your water tray by blowing your sails.

What's in it for the children?

Again, this is another great way of combining exploration of materials and how they behave with water play. It is ideal for building on and challenging children's understanding of floating and sinking as well as playing with forces as they blow their boats around.

Coloured paint ice cubes

What you need:

- **A couple of cans of shaving cream** (hypo allergenic if you have children with sensitive skin)
- **Ice cube tray**
- **Food colouring**
- **Access to a freezer**
- **A large shallow tray** (a gravel or builder's tray is ideal)

What to do:

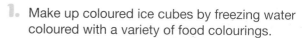

1. Make up coloured ice cubes by freezing water coloured with a variety of food colourings.
2. Take your tray outside and cover the surface with swirls of shaving cream, the more the better.
3. When frozen tip the ice cubes into the shaving cream and spread around.
4. Encourage the children to explore moving the coloured cubes around in the shaving cream, mixing the colours and making shapes.

Taking it forward

- Try freezing poster paint and using this instead of frozen water.
- Explore coloured ice cubes in other materials such as sand or water.
- Try freezing small objects into the cubes so children can find them as they melt. Add sparkles and glitter for even more excitement.

What's in it for the children?

This is a great way of integrating early science exploration of materials onto a multi-sensory messy play exploration. Not only do children explore ice melting, and colours mixing but they use plenty of descriptive language as they play. Children also develop their fine motor skills as they explore moving the cubes around (great for those all important pre-writing skills).

Top tip ⭐

Try freezing a little coloured water and them adding a different colour and re-freezing to make rainbow cubes.

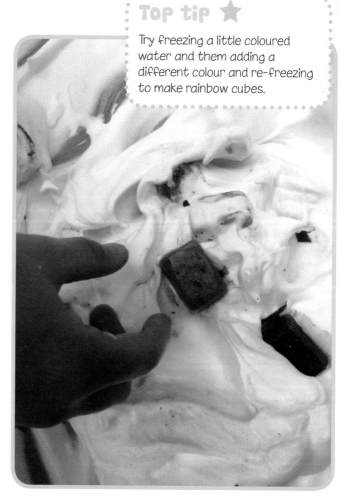